The Wanderer's Prayer
&
The Travel Log
of Sofa Joe

Other Publications:

Ode to a BiC Biro, after Wittgenstein (Trombone Press, 1996)
The Sleep Switch (Odyssey Poets, 1996)
West of Yesterday (Stride, 1998)
Vital Movement (contributor, Reality Street Editions, 1999)

As Editor:

Binary Myths (Stride, 1998) Conversations with contemporary poets.
Binary Myths 2 (Stride, 1999) Correspondences with poet-editors.

The Wanderer's Prayer
&
The Travel Log
of Sofa Joe

ANDY BROWN

PUBLICATIONS

Published by Arc Publications
Nanholme Mill, Shaw Wood Road
Todmorden, Lancs. OL14 6DA

Design by Tony Ward
Printed by Arc & Throstle Press
Nanholme Mill, Todmorden, Lancs.

ISBN 1 900072 32 7

Cover illustration: *The Fool Puts to Sea in an Untrustworthy Ship,* by Albrecht Dürer (1494)

The publishers acknowledge financial assistance from Yorkshire Arts Board

for my parents
Ruth and Dereke

THE WANDERER'S PRAYER

"...in a post-modern night-club you can get laughed at
for mentioning anything that might be misconstrued
as Odyssey, Quest, Pilgrimage or Mission Impossible.
They've all got such big capital letters."

Paul Hyland

I

The footsteps of god is the mythical spot where the river leaves the mountains on its long & varied journey over land towards the sea. Woodland channels, barrages & buildings rise riparian. Walkways bridge these peopled plots.

A god left the soles of his feet pressed in the rocks & that's why people gather here & candles float downstream to drums & music. Leave your shoes by the door, leave your feet by the door, drink & dive & light a candle. We are here to see what we can never see & are ourselves in doing so seen –

> sightseer, holy man, beggar-man, priest,
> swannee whistler, drink stall holder,
> women selling rice balloons

– a multitude at the water's edge, to drink, to bathe, to swim, to pray, to ask for health & a life that moves & as light fades & the sun stops sun-ness, priests swing incense burning brands, ring gongs & bells & inner space expands to fill the head with earth-fire-water-sky, the air, the sounds that air can hold

         a
        mo
        ment

& the crowd begin singing
   & people dive in
      & all the candled boats embark
         & set off on the swirling eddies
            & buying a boat, we remove our shoes
               & go down to the river's edge
               & by the side we stop
                  & enter with our feet
               & wash our foreheads
                  & our hands
                     & think of family
                  & friends
                     & push the fragile vessel out
                        & watch it disappear

this little *Ulysses* of a prayer on its roundabout tour to
& from its origins.

      ❦

II

The morning's open, random light
falls on *The City of Dreadful Night*.
Rising with the blanket smog, names on names,
a pantheon of scientists & poets, ordered in the mind –

Calcutta has just thrown up a street named *Shakespeare*,
Kipling, *Thackery*, the family *Tagore*, Rabindranath's
                                        Gitanjali
& one more Nobel Prize for the man who found out
the mosquito's secret – Sir Ronald Ross.

This is the oldest culture left on Earth.
It's only right to think about these scientists & poets,
physicists who are now further into black holes,
getting into Tao – about the pantheistic masses

living in its shit & stink; this order in the
chaos that's a journey through this city,
its all too human lot; the ever present sound
of singing 'rituals bring us closer to god.'

&

III

High on a crest in a car that climbs by wires in breeze &
view, the hills splay wide like toes of the imagination.
Birds take to the sky, in which the mountains nest, as
sparks of light...

❦

IV

We are right up in the clouds & can't see far. The valley
has filled with mist. Monkeys squabble on the rooftops.
The thrum of cicadas & grasshoppers. Twilight. Electric
noise. Those TV speakers. In the distance, lorry horns –
a sleepless nightmare of an all day journey. Windows
sparking up across the night...

❧

V

Macchapuchhare
Sagarmatha
the names roll off each other
like mountains.

The peninsula
presses into the mainland
& they rise like two hands
joined in *Namaste*.

Up there, uncluttered & utterly
alone, you can see
their reflections sink
through mountain pools.

❦

VI

Blueing
away
into distance.

Waiting.
A moment
of transit.

Each shadow
leaves
casting a flower.

❦

VII

Descending from the humid mists, the plains glide under the mountains. On a hard seat in sweating heat, for the hours it takes to get us back, we sit in wooden carriages, crossing rivers, holy rivers, throw in coins, watch buffalo bathing, share bananas, snips of talk. Our travelling companion shows us icons; thinks we are on pilgrimage; can't connect us to this place – "What will you *do* here for five days?"

❧

VIII

"Are you simply tourists here,
or do you spiritually aspire?
Are you only sightseers,
or budding devotees?"

If you mean, do I desire
to swap my schedule, my route,
this routine getting away from routine
which we call holiday, for robes
& getting higher by chanting god's name,
I see all of this & more & yes,
I'm just another traveller.

Where is there to go, once
you've been here in yourself?

IX

The driver sits beneath the tree
smoking hashish while it rains.

Passing through roads that are
rivers, in a bus that's a boat –

you're not the one who takes it,
it takes you.

X

From bus dismount – it is as if we have ourselves been sensed arriving from five miles back & the taxis become magnetised to our northern poles. Our companion is trying to say something, maybe "I'll come with you," but eyes and hands don't translate into any other language & we speed off wondering what will become of him; if our times will cross again; if we will be perceived as we wish to be perceived. Relief contains some shred of vanity.

❧

XI

This building is light & fragrant –
it lies outside the nexus of the town.
The roads to it are lined with snarling dogs.
The floor has cool smooth stones.
The sun shoots off these polished rocks.
The desert stretches far away & groans.

Within the gates we find the gardens.
Passing through the low-slung pathways,
mazes of bougainvillaea
& steps that lead to various chambers,
tunnelled walkways, inlayed walls,
below us now – the lake.

Vultures circle the edifice effortlessly.
We are at the mercy of our bodies
with their cycles & functions.
On the other side of a door
with an elephant carved into a handle,
colourful women sell fruit.

You perfect walls,
how shall we live between you,
but eat delicious oranges & nuts?

❧

XII

If you asked a Hopi Indian I believe they would call you *Earth Mother*. A Cretan or Minoan vision sees you as a goddess. In Russia, Egypt & Peru, I have heard them speak of you in the same breath as coins, caves & graves –

but *this* ancient culture worships you for your one times light, your nine times darkness.

Labyrinth.

XIII

We start again. A net of lanes. These webs of stairwells
overlooked by terracotta figurines. A beautiful woman
by a pile of pots: you in cotton head-scarf. The European-
ness of it all – the rain, more rain, the coffee shop, the
sprung umbrellas, Le Courbusier. A tourist shooting
film on Ayurvedic medicine.

ॐ

XIV

Pilgrims & worshippers walk the paths into the hills through marijuana forests. Plastic gods, gaudy paintings, a buy buy buy & pray pray pray, where the money mantra rings all day with: 'The Soap of the Stars', a famous balm, superior joss, washing bars, mango sweeties, "very good quality toilet paper" & discrete condoms – a couple stroll into the sunset overhung by the words 'Make Love Not Babies'.

☙

XV

Recurring man.
Eyes to melt mountains.

We cannot talk & so we'll smile
& share belongings:

you, a prayer mat;
us, an inflatable travel pillow.

❧

XVI

A porter like a tortoise
with a wardrobe on his back.
He stops to rest as we pass by –

"What else can I do?
Man proposes, God disposes.
What else can I do?"

❧

XVII

Strange to be back, but this time it's raining, cooling the air & softening the marble underfoot – a freshwater 'teardrop on the face of eternity'. Throwing flowers into the symmetry, he cries fresh tears. The echoes sound like whale song.

20,000 people working every day, for 22 years, for one man's grief.

❧

XVIII

We boarded a boat that took us through lagoons banked
by palms, fishing nets hoisted on cranes, like praying
mantis' legs, high above the waters & the villages which
fish them. The scene conjured up Conrad's *Heart Of
Darkness*; Coppola's *Apocalypse Now*. But ours was no
soul rending dark trip. We were not wending our way
to meet some Kurtz, although I reached a passage in the
book I was reading about fear – primitive respect. Two
of the characters were painfully you & I. I then became
aware of the power behind the boat.

❧

XIX

Watching haul go from mesh to dugout,
death owns the catch for necessity.

Trawled opals. They are cold. Indifferent. Quick
fingers free the dying from the nets & boat them.
They do not suffocate as sweetly as we drown.

Before relaunch & cast, the inedible fish
are sifted out, buried in sand scoops above the tide.

The small fry are shared out as gifts,
carried by children in silver tubs
through huts with herring-bone roofs.

They await a limbo on bamboo
poles, sunning into leather.

Along the cackling barnyard paths,
dogs & goats hoover prawn heads,
discarded shells. Nothing goes to waste.

❦

XX

Voices ascend the slippery shore –
this tomb in the seaweed's fetters.
We need only praise
the starfish for constancy.

Silence adorns these islands' coasts
with fugitive joys in huts & palm trees.
The waking fish are snagged
from a tide carving papery neaps

& colonise the olive dullness
wallowing where Hosannas once pulsed.
The wave shadows. The thirst persists.
We leap along lost boulevards of trees.

XXI

We walk along a long-gone riverbed
through a village where children, hoopoes,
peacocks & green bee-eaters skirt around
the carcass ground – flocks of vultures,

ripped up camels, cows & asses, buffalo.
The dogs roam freely, sticking heads in
right down to the collar bone. Cages, skulls
& vertebrae litter the grass. A man is paid to take care
                                                    of it all.

❧

XXII

A squad of uniformed shy girls,
with coloured pie-sliced parasols,
stir the day back to simplicity.
Their colours gel & twist inside.
The whole effect is humorous,
trying to dance in step & time
to *Roll Out The Barrel* on the grass,
between a marble monument
to the Raj & a shit-filled ditch.
They miss their steps. They're honest kids.
They're in rehearsal for something big.

The market too has flowers.
I study its narrowing alleys.
Stray dogs run between the banks
of blooms & butchers' slabs in front.
Both have a graspable life. We pass
one dog by, skin peeled well off
the bone. Eyes out. Agog. A sweet,
sickening smell on the pavement
outside Ronald Ross' malaria lab.
On the wall, his epitaph: 'I find thy
cunning seed, O million murdering death.'

XXIII

You don't have to understand
you *can* do here; you simply *do*.

You have no reason
to do otherwise.

In this huge universe of a thing
you simply come a little closer.

❧

NOTES

The title of the poem comes from a line in *The Odyssey, Book V*.

The epigram comes from *Backwards Out Of The Big World*, by Paul Hyland.

1. **The River Ganges** at Haridwar, Northern India.

2. **The City of Dreadful Night** (Kipling), about Calcutta.

   Rabindranath Tagore's *Gitanjali: Song Offerings* were free verse recreations of his Bengali poems, modelled on devotional Indian lyrics, that won the Nobel Prize for literature in 1913.

   In Calcutta, **Sir Ronald Ross** discovered that the female Anopheles mosquito was the carrier of the Malaria virus. He was awarded the Nobel Prize for his work. Ross was also a poet. (See note for 22.)

5. **Macchapuchhare**, The Fish-Tail Mountain in the Nepalese Himalayas.

   Sagarmatha, Mount Everest in the Nepalese Himalayas.

   Namaste, Hindu & Nepalese greeting, meaning literally *'I salute everything that is great in you'*.

13 **Le Courbusier**, the European architect who designed Chandigarh, capital city of the Punjab.

17. **Rabindranath Tagore** writing about the Taj Mahal, mausoleum for the body of the wife of Shah Jahan. Shah Jahan was later imprisoned in the Red Fort at Agra, by his son, and gazed over at the Taj Mahal every day from his prison across the river.

20. The state of **Kerala** has a recent Christian history.

22. **"I find thy cunning seed, O million murdering death"**, from Sir Ronald Ross' poem about the discovery of the malaria virus.

THE TRAVEL LOG OF SOFA JOE

DAY ONE

Light.

Sleep.

The Desert.

Day One then Day Two.
Annihilating opposites.

With my religious temperament
but lack of religious conviction
I began to read 'Religious Thought
Beyond the Limits of Imagination.'

Fell asleep. The ruined city.
Woke up at the bottom of a moving river.
Somebody was playing god by playing
A song called 'Here Comes Immortality' –

it was spiritual murder through suggestion.

DAY TWO

I am the root who makes us two.
Two are the roots that grow the tree.
Three is the tree with its life of leaves
floating between the yellow lands of day
& the bluer lands of night.

Who is experiencing this...?
Who is experiencing this *at this time* ...?
Where were you when...?
Did you do the...?
Have you seen the...?
etc...etc...

Apart from that today was not a day
to remember – a void beneath the bridge.

DAY THREE

Three people & the objects in a room.
The form that's made by distances between them.

1. Three people in a simple setting **X**, **Y** & **Z**.
2. One event which binds them.
3. Each with their personal opinion about the event & each other.
4. **X** believes.
   Y an obsessive distrust of **X**.
   Z understands **Y**, sympathises with **X**, though holding no belief
   themself.
5. **X** an enthusiasm to convince **Z** & an understanding of **Y**.
   Y annoyed with **X** & **Z** for condescension & pluralism alike.
   Z knows **Y** is intolerant & **X** wasting their time here.
6. The inescapable triangle.
7. A discussion about 'dreaming' over dinner.

DAY FOUR

It has been scientifically proven
we've a problem today
in digesting the point of our souls –
Dyspepsia of the Biblical Passage.

They've also proved that I am not
physiologically the same person as I
appeared to be this morning – sleep & waking
hormones are completely different.

I shift through this shifting reality like sand.

DAY FIVE

Is it not I
who lives out these fictions?

I am
an endangered being.

DAY SIX

Waking to find myself as someone else
walking to the guillotine. Cathartic.
Fell asleep before the cutter fell.
This overriding quest for love. Still stuck.

DAY SEVEN

This is my palimpsest.
I discovered the original lying
on the road to the ruined city.
Liking the look of the parchment
I erased the content for my own.
The ruins were sterile
& silent & made me
tread quietly.
Fallen civilisations
have this effect on me.

THE ORIGINAL

Organic Remains – Mythology – Landscape
Roots – Ruins – Ancients
Origins – Ends
Children – Needs – Ritual
Preservation – Inheritance
...a whole paragraph of smudges...
...something about Identity & Desire...
Metamorphosis – Mirrors
Decoration & Magic
Perspective – Displacement
Recognition
The Road

DAY EIGHT

I woke up in the station feeling crucified.
Usually the station is essential
(a palace where stories continue)
but there the hailer system harassed
me with the hubbub of masses.

Thanks to the abstract for saving
me from the guilt of compassion.

DAY NINE

The onanistic onus of that past –
selfish & self-satisfied
& not as good as the real thing
& not as real as the good thing.

DAY TEN

& people shall have no opinion
'Dead men naked they shall be one...
Though lovers be lost Love shall not'
& people shall have their opinion.

DAY ELEVEN

A saint flying by on a frog.
A devil with a basket picking souls.
A poet stealing bones of words for dogs.
The Nothingness that is desired & loathed –

why hope for return
when this is what
you'll come back to?

What faces us now is History, not hysterics.
By sophisticated usury & the usual sophistry
they disintegrate our dreams.

DAY TWELVE

This city is a mystery. Grotesque.
The crowd's identity masks
the character of this place.
Will I continue to want
to postpone my identity?

There is a person (anonymous) aiming
to recognise themselves in a shop window.
There is another trying to realise
themselves in the book of their city.
Here is someone actually thanking god
for expelling us from Paradise.

Somebody voices themselves in the void.
They slip from the pavement & go down...

DAYS THIRTEEN TO TWENTY-NINE

There are no entries
for these days.

DAY THIRTY

This landscape leads you through extremes;
makes you make judgements
you would do best to forget.

Monkeys fill its trees
& dry slopes with their riddles.
Their insatiable hunger. Their threats.

DAY THIRTY-ONE

Where I have been
& what I have seen

have become words
& words have become

where others go
what others see.

This life cannot be told
apart from words.

To understand this
mirrored place –

see yours in mine
& mine in your face.

DAY THIRTY-TWO

Getting There. Being There. Staying.
For the eyes' ears.
For the things I cannot name.
For the things I'd love to paint.

DAY THIRTY-THREE

Sunrise for breakfast.
Sunsets for tea.
When will this stop
feeding me?